23/08/2024

MY EXPERIENCE IN THE CHARISMATIC MOVEMENT

William Myers

Please use the information in this manuscript in any way you see fit. Brother Perry Cotham had me write this book for the benefit of others. He served as more than just a brother in Christ. He was my second earthly father. After my father died, he became my sounding board. He begged me to take over his work in India. I did so for a decade, and then the money ran out. Very few men have impacted so many people like Brother Perry. I miss him and look forward to the day we can sit together in paradise.

Bill Myers is a faithful gospel preacher. He has given to the brotherhood a valuable book which deserves a wide distribution in all parts of the world. Those who read this book with an honest and sincere heart will benefit greatly from it. We predict it will be a great influence for good for the Lord's church.

■ *Perry B. Cotham*

MY EXPERIENCE IN THE CHARISMATIC MOVEMENT

Contents

A BRIEF HISTORY

INTRODUCTION

The Charismatic Movement encompasses a variety of groups and denominations within Christianity, each emphasizing the work of the Holy Spirit and the exercise of spiritual gifts. While these groups share common themes, they differ in their practices, theological emphases, and organizational structures. This document outlines several key charismatic groups, highlighting their historical development and contributions to the broader Charismatic Movement.

Pentecostal Churches

Assemblies of God

- **Origins and History:** Founded in 1914, the Assemblies of God is one of the largest and most influential Pentecostal denominations globally. It emerged from the Pentecostal revival that began in the early 20th century, particularly the Azusa Street Revival.

- **Distinctive Features:** The Assemblies of God emphasizes the Baptism in the Holy Spirit, evidenced by speaking in tongues. It also stresses the practice of spiritual gifts, divine healing, and evangelism.

- **Impact:** The Assemblies of God has significantly spread Pentecostalism worldwide and influenced other charismatic and evangelical groups.

Church of God (Cleveland, Tennessee)

- **Origins and History:** Established in 1886, the Church of God (Cleveland, Tennessee) is another major Pentecostal denomination. It grew out of the holiness movement and the early Pentecostal revival.

- **Distinctive Features:** The Church of God emphasizes Baptism in the Holy Spirit, speaking in tongues, and the operation of spiritual gifts. It also focuses on holiness and Christ's imminent return.

- **Impact:** This denomination has contributed to the global expansion of Pentecostalism and has influenced various charismatic and evangelical movements.

Pentecostal Holiness Church

- **Origins and History:** The Pentecostal Holiness Church was formed in 1898 by merging several Pentecostal and holiness groups. It is a significant player in the Pentecostal movement.

- **Distinctive Features:** The church emphasizes the experience of Baptism in the Holy Spirit, speaking in tongues, and divine healing. It also upholds the holiness tradition.

- **Impact:** The Pentecostal Holiness Church has been instrumental in promoting Pentecostal theology and practice, particularly in the southeastern United States.

Charismatic Renewal Movements
Catholic Charismatic Renewal

Origins and History: The Catholic Charismatic Renewal begin in the late 1960s, influenced by the broader Charismatic Movement. The Duquesne Weekend in 1967 was a pivotal event that marked the movement's emergence within the Roman Catholic Church.

- **Distinctive Features:** The movement emphasizes the active presence of the Holy Spirit, including spiritual gifts such as speaking in tongues and prophecy. It also integrates Catholic traditions with charismatic practices.

- **Impact:** The Catholic Charismatic Renewal has revitalized Catholic worship and spirituality, fostering ecumenical dialogue and influencing Catholic practice worldwide.

Renewal Movements within Mainline Protestantism

- **Origins and History:** Various mainline Protestant denominations, including the Episcopal Church, the Lutheran Church, and the Methodist Church, experienced charismatic renewal in the 1960s and 1970s.

- **Distinctive Features:** These renewal movements emphasize the experience of the Holy Spirit and spiritual gifts within traditional mainline frameworks.

They often seek to balance charismatic practices with historical liturgical traditions.

- **Impact:** Charismatic renewal within mainline denominations has led to the formation of charismatic congregations and influenced the broader mainline Protestant landscape.

Vineyard Movement

- **Origins and History:** Founded by John Wimber in the 1980s, the Vineyard Movement emerged from the broader Charismatic Movement and emphasized practical applications of charismatic gifts.

- **Distinctive Features:** The Vineyard Movement focuses on the experiential aspects of the Holy Spirit, including healing, prophecy, and worship. It also emphasizes a relaxed, informal style of worship and outreach.

- **Impact:** The Vineyard Movement has influenced contemporary worship practices and contributed to the global spread of charismatic Christianity.

Independent Charismatic Churches

The Toronto Airport Vineyard Church

Origins and History: The Toronto Airport Vineyard Church, led by John and Carol Arnott, gained prominence in the 1990s due to the Toronto Blessing, a significant charismatic revival.

- **Distinctive Features:** The Toronto Blessing is known for its manifestations of the Holy Spirit, including laughter, shaking, and other physical phenomena. The church emphasizes the experiential aspects of charismatic worship.

- **Impact:** The Toronto Airport Vineyard Church has had a global impact, inspiring similar movements and influencing charismatic and Pentecostal churches worldwide.

Bethel Church (Redding, California)

- **Origins and History:** Founded by Bill Johnson, Bethel Church in Redding, California, has become a prominent charismatic church known for its focus on supernatural ministry and revival.

- **Distinctive Features:** Bethel Church emphasizes healing, prophecy, and miracles. It also promotes a culture of revival and supernatural encounters, emphasizing worship and spiritual growth.

- **Impact:** Bethel Church has influenced contemporary charismatic practices and worship through its music ministry and online presence.

The Charismatic Movement encompasses diverse groups and denominations, each contributing to the broader understanding and practice of charismatic Christianity. From Pentecostal churches with early roots in the 20th-century revivals to charismatic renewal movements within mainline denominations, the movement reflects a dynamic and evolving expression of Christian faith. Independent charismatic churches, such as the Toronto Airport Vineyard Church and Bethel Church, continue to shape contemporary worship and spirituality.

Infiltrating the Churches of Christ

The Charismatic Movement, emphasizing the presence of the Holy Spirit and spiritual gifts, has had a notable impact on various Christian denominations. This document explores the movement's influence on the Churches of Christ, examining how these distinct traditions have interacted, the points of contention, and the instances of integration or resistance. Understanding this influence provides insight into the dynamic interplay between charismatic practices and traditional Church of Christ beliefs.

The Churches of Christ, a group within the Restoration Movement, emphasize a return to New Testament Christianity, focusing on scriptural authority, simplicity in worship, and a distinct absence of overt charismatic practices. The Charismatic Movement, in contrast, highlights the active experience of the Holy Spirit, including the exercise of spiritual gifts such as speaking in tongues and prophecy. The interaction between these two traditions has been marked by tension and adaptation.

Background of the Charismatic Movement

Origins and Key Characteristics

The Charismatic Movement emerged in the early 20th century, emphasizing the active presence of the Holy Spirit and the practice of spiritual gifts. Influenced by Pentecostalism, the movement is characterized by its focus on supernatural experiences, including speaking in tongues, prophecy, healing, and miracles. Key events such as the Azusa Street Revival (1906) and subsequent charismatic revivals set the stage for the movement's spread across various Christian denominations.

Theological Emphases

Central to the Charismatic Movement is the belief in the Baptism conversion. This experience is often evidenced by speaking in tongues and other charismatic manifestations. The movement also emphasizes the continuity of spiritual gifts and the expectation of miraculous signs as part of the Christian experience.

Overview of the Churches of Christ

Historical and Theological Background

The Churches of Christ trace their roots to the Restoration Movement of the early 19th century, which sought to restore the practices and doctrines of the New Testament church. Emphasizing scriptural authority, weekly observance of the Lord's Supper, and a cappella singing, the Churches of Christ maintain a conservative approach to worship and theology.

Beliefs and Practices

Fundamental beliefs in the Churches of Christ include the importance of baptism by immersion for the remission of sins, the autonomy of the local congregation, and the rejection of instrumental music in worship. The movement generally avoids charismatic practices, focusing instead on adherence to New Testament teachings and maintaining doctrinal purity.

Infiltration and Influence of the Charismatic Movement

Early Interactions and Responses

Introducing charismatic elements into Churches of Christ congregations has often been resisted. Traditional members and leaders typically view charismatic practices as deviations from scriptural teachings. Early attempts to integrate charismatic practices, such as speaking in tongues or prophecy, were generally rejected by mainstream Churches of Christ, which emphasized maintaining traditional practices and theological boundaries.

Examples of Charismatic Influence

Despite resistance, there have been instances where charismatic practices have found their way into Churches of Christ. Some congregations have adopted aspects of charismatic worship, including more expressive forms of prayer and contemporary worship styles. Additionally, individuals influenced by charismatic beliefs have occasionally joined or impacted congregations, leading to a blending of practices.

Case Studies

- **The Impact of Revival Movements:** Some Churches of Christ congregations have experienced charismatic influences through revival movements and charismatic preachers. These movements sometimes introduce charismatic practices during special services or events, leading to varying acceptance or conflict within the congregation.

- **Influence of Individual Leaders:** Charismatic leaders within the Churches of Christ occasionally promote charismatic practices, creating tension with traditional members and leaders. These individuals may emphasize personal spiritual experiences and seek to integrate charismatic elements into the church's worship and ministry.

Points of Contention and Conflict

Theological Discrepancies

The primary point of contention between the Charismatic Movement and the Churches of Christ lies in the theological understanding of spiritual gifts and the role of the Holy Spirit. The Churches of Christ typically reject the notion of ongoing miraculous gifts, viewing them as having ceased with the completion of the New Testament canon. In contrast, the Charismatic Movement views these gifts as active and relevant for contemporary believers.

Worship Practices

The inclusion of charismatic practices, such as spontaneous prayer, speaking in tongues, and physical manifestations, often conflicts with the structured and traditional worship practices of the Churches of Christ. Using contemporary worship styles influenced by charismatic practices can also lead to disputes over the appropriate form and content of worship.

Ecclesiastical Autonomy

The autonomous nature of Churches of Christ congregations means that responses to charismatic influences can vary widely. Some congregations may embrace elements of charismatic worship, while others may strongly oppose such practices, leading to internal divisions and debates.

Adaptations and Integration

The Emergence of Charismatic Elements

In some instances, Churches of Christ have adapted to charismatic influences by incorporating elements of contemporary worship that align with charismatic practices. These adaptations may include more expressive forms of worship but typically do not fully embrace the broader spectrum of charismatic practices.

Balancing Tradition and Innovation

Some congregations have sought to balance traditional Church of Christ practices with contemporary charismatic influences, focusing on integrating worship styles without compromising core theological beliefs. This approach allows for innovation while maintaining adherence to traditional principles.

The influence of the Charismatic Movement on the Churches of Christ has been marked by resistance and adaptation. While traditional Churches of Christ have maintained mainly their conservative approach to worship and theology, charismatic practices have occasionally found their way into congregations, leading to varying degrees of integration and conflict. Understanding this dynamic interaction provides insight into the broader landscape of charismatic Christianity and how different Christian traditions navigate theological and practical differences.

The interaction between charismatic practices and the Churches of Christ highlights the challenges and opportunities of integrating diverse expressions of faith within a tradition committed to scriptural authority and historical continuity. As the Charismatic Movement continues to evolve, its influence on the Churches of Christ and other traditional Christian groups will remain an ongoing area of interest and examination.

INTRODUCTION

I remember the day my daughter was born. My first thought was, "I am truly blessed!" God had entrusted me with a precious little girl, and I knew my mission was to guide her to heaven. I never imagined being blessed with six wonderful children who would show more faithfulness to the church in their early years than I ever did.

It wasn't that I was ignorant or raised to reject the church. Though not as active as they could have been, my parents were not the cause of my drifting away from the Kingdom. The reasons for my departure are recorded in the pages that follow.

This book offers a firsthand look into the charismatic movement, a powerful wave that swept across this country in the 1960s and 70s. It was an experience that has left an indelible mark on my life. While I am deeply grateful to be in God's Kingdom now, a part of me still mourns the many friends I left behind.

It's not that I wish to be part of that movement again. Instead, I have a deep conviction that I once led many astray friends who trusted me, only to be guided into darkness, never showing them the true light.

I continue to pray for them, hoping that a gospel preacher will someday knock on their door. But if not, I fear their chances of finding the truth are slim.

As ministers of the gospel, we must recognize the urgent need to spread the truth to the earth's four corners. So many are blinded by false teachings, their minds perverted by lies. We must lead them out of darkness and into the light. This, and this alone, is the purpose behind unveiling my past.

INTRODUCTION

Imagine standing on the bank of the Jordan River during the first year of the Lord's ministry. You see a large crowd gathered as you gaze toward a small hillside near the shore. Curiosity draws you up the hillside, where you find a young man preaching to the multitude. After His sermon, you follow along with the crowd. Suddenly, an elderly woman, afflicted with a severe blood disease, reaches out and touches the hem of His garment. Miraculously, she is made whole. Astonishingly, others plead with the young man to heal their ailments. Before your eyes, the blind receive their sight, the lame walk, and the mute speak. Deep within your heart, you realize this is no ordinary man; this is indeed the Son of God.

"If it happened long ago, why not now?" This is the logical conclusion that leads many to embrace the charismatic philosophy. They believe witnessing a miracle proves their faith is not in vain. Sadly, once convinced they have seen a miracle, these individuals become nearly impossible to convert to the truth. It requires knowledge and skill to reach those still willing to listen.

However, every soul is precious. Even if many refuse to hear the gospel, never give up! It would be best if you believed that somewhere, someone is beginning to question what they've been taught. This is the person searching for a way out. I know this because I was once one of those individuals. I thank God that His light shone in my direction!

I begin this book by sharing what it was like to be part of the charismatic movement. My goal is to provide insight into their theology and, with kindness and love, show you how to guide others out of darkness and into the light.

CHAPTER ONE

I. RECEIVING THE HOLY SPIRIT

It was my first year in college. I had just entered my freshman year at Vincennes University in Vincennes, Indiana. Like most young freshmen attending their first semester, I was looking for a way to meet new friends. Being a member of the church of Christ, I started attending the congregation in Vincennes. The brethren were friendly, and in the beginning, I attended several of their youth gatherings.

I was proud of myself. I, for the first time in my life, had a zeal to do that which was right. I tried never to miss services or any special events that were associated with the church. However, my faith was soon to detour from the proper path.

Strolling back to my dormitory after lunch one day, I heard a conversation going on between several young students. The subject they were discussing was the Holy Spirit. Once I entered the open door to the room where the discussion was being held, I offered an apology for my intrusion. "No sweat!" Bob replied, "come on in and join in our discussion."

I never thought that the moment I entered that open door, the door of truth would be shut for ten years. I loved the brethren at Vincennes, but I was a teenager who desperately needed friends my own age. Hence, I felt that Bob and his colleagues were the answer to all my problems. Face it! Most

17

of the creatures on this planet thirst for attention and friendship, especially a young college student like me who had been feeling the plague of loneliness. Looking back, I wish I could have remained introverted.

"Why leave the church?" I have had people ask me on several occasions. The first time I entered the door to Bob's room, I heard things I was not capable of refuting. The subject of the Holy Spirit was something I knew nothing about, yet Bob made it seem so easy. Not only that but also, I felt comfortable around people my own age. I finally had friends. We would all go to breakfast together and stay up many nights talking about the Bible. Truthfully, I wanted to be entertained, pampered. When I was introduced to the Charismatic movement in the fall of 1973 that need was fulfilled. By comparison, the church of Christ could not compete with my new-found friends, and new-found religion. I didn't want to participate. The preaching was boring. There seemed to be very few activities for young people, and I just didn't see the need to be faithful. In that small dormitory room at Vincennes University, I would begin a journey leading me further from the truth- so far, indeed, that the way back home seemed almost impossible.

1. "Rose to Play"

A verse in the book of Exodus reads, "And the people sat down to eat and to drink and rose up to play" (Exodus 32:6).

This passage concerns itself with the wrongful attitude of the Israelites and personifies the charismatic religion. Most of those whom I knew within the movement were emotional fanatics. The guitars, drums, and having fun enticed many of us that we had found the proper way to heaven. After all, why shouldn't services be entertaining?

Unfortunately, sitting and listening to someone open a Bible and preach for thirty minutes is boring for most people. My misunderstanding of the meaning of worship and my childlike demeanor caused me to despise attending services.

2. A Grand Entertainer

One of the finest speakers I ever encountered was a young college student from Bowling Green University. Raised in the Pentecostal tradition, his charisma was nothing short of astonishing. With his strong voice and good looks, he effortlessly charmed most of the ladies on campus during his brief visit. His reason for being there was to see his girlfriend, who happened to be part of our small group. She was a dedicated follower of the movement's philosophies and deeply loved Peter.

Peter was not ordinary; he had been standing in pulpits since junior high school. He was dynamic, a natural orator whose smooth speeches and humorous stories captivated everyone. His mesmerizing abilities, however, led me one step further from God.

2. Time to Receive the Spirit

It was a beautiful evening outside the classroom, during which Peter conducted one of his final sessions before returning to Bowling Green University. His topic was the Holy Spirit, but this time, he emphasized the identifiable marks of a true believer in Christ. Peter explained that salvation could not be obtained unless one received the baptismal measure of the Holy Spirit and began to speak in tongues. He quoted passages commonly cited by Pentecostals—John 14:16, 26; 15:26; Acts 2; Acts 10:46; 19:6; 1 Corinthians 12:10—verses that convinced my soul I needed to receive what Peter said God was so willing to give.

After the lesson, Peter led his faithful followers to the basement of one of the dormitories. The laundry room became our gathering place, where an extraordinary event was about to unfold. Standing in the middle of the room, Peter asked if anyone wanted to receive the Holy Spirit. I, along with two others, stepped forward. To the charismatic, this was the seal of salvation. I liked it more than anything.

I vividly remember Peter laying his hands on the first candidate, who soon began to utter words—if you could call them that! Then he moved to the second candidate, and after a brief hesitation, they, too, began to speak in tongues. Finally, it was my turn. My stomach churned with a mix of nerves and excitement. "What if he lays his hands on me and nothing happens? What will my new friends think?" The questions swirled in my mind, soon to be answered.

When Peter laid his hands on me the first time, nothing happened. I felt strange, unsettled. There was no power surge, no miraculous sign of the Holy Spirit's presence. The crowd began to whisper. Some claimed Satan was preventing me from accepting the Spirit, while others spoke in tongues, seemingly offering prayers on my behalf. Peter touched me a second time. Still, nothing happened. I could see the frustration in Peter's eyes. The voices of friends cheering me on filled the room.

Peter laid his hands on me a third and final time. Desperate, I thought to myself, "Make it happen!" I began to fake it, uttering nonsensical sounds and words. I knew I was fabricating the entire experience, but I heard only laughter and praise in the background. "Hallelujah!" one man proclaimed. "Praise God!" echoed another.

That night, as I returned to the dorm, I stopped by the room of one of my new brothers. I confessed to him that I had faked the entire experience. He looked deep into my eyes and assured me that what had happened was real. He explained that Satan was causing me to doubt, and then, raising his voice, he declared, "The Spirit within me has informed me that you are filled with His presence." He added, "I have the Spirit of interpretation and understood everything you said." I was stunned. What could I say? Could it be true? Was it Satan's deception that led me to question everything? The more I thought about it, the more I convinced myself he was right. In the end, I walked out of that room a charismatic.

After several more Bible studies, my new brothers and sisters began helping me practice speaking in tongues. Over time, I learned to turn the utterances on and off whenever and wherever I liked. By this point, all my doubts about the movement were behind me. Nothing was more important than attending the meetings and keeping the faith. This, as far as I was concerned, was true religion. Where else could one attend services filled with fun, games, pleasure, and uplifting entertainment? Looking back at my days in the church of Christ, I realized how boring and shallow their services seemed. No bands were playing to excite the spirit, no choirs or entertainers to capture the people's attention. All they had was the truth.

The beautiful thing about truth is that "the truth shall make you free" (John 8:32). But I was not accessible under this new religion. Sure, something new was always happening, but even that eventually became old. I was being led with a chain around my neck. However, when I began questioning leaders' actions confidently, that chain was pulled even tighter.

The charismatic world is a controlled environment. The leaders have a firm grip on everything within the group, making it difficult for anyone to grasp the truth. Occasionally, the truth finds its way into the heart of a charismatic, but it is quickly plucked out by one of the more vital members of the community.

People often call charismatics ignorant, but this is not necessarily true. Many within the group are highly educated and diligent in their studies. Although they frequently draw the wrong conclusions about many things, it does not negate their zeal to learn the Bible. Initially, the closeness of the group is what attracts most people to the movement. However, in the end, this closeness can become more of a hindrance than an asset. The truth is that people don't want to be entirely controlled by others; they desire at least a certain amount of freedom. So, it rubs many the wrong way when they are told what they can or cannot do.

True Christianity is based on the concept of free moral choice. We become slaves to Christ not because we are forced to but because we choose to. Therefore, the charismatic philosophy of controlling the group makes the religion a cult.

1. Born of the Spirit

"Verily, verily, I say unto thee, Except a man be born of water and of the Spirit, he cannot enter into the kingdom of God" (John 3:5). These words from the immortal Savior to Nicodemus, a "ruler of the Jews" (John 3:1), were meant to impart a profound lesson about the kingdom of God. In my early years in the charismatic movement, I believed this verse taught that the baptism of the Holy Spirit was promised to all believers. However, I later learned that this interpretation was incorrect.

Baptism is a fascinating study, with several types mentioned in the Bible: the baptism of fire (Matthew 3:11), the baptism of the Holy Spirit (Matthew 3:11), the baptism for the dead (1 Corinthians 15:29), and water baptism (Matthew 3:16; Mark 16:16; Acts 2:38; 8:36-38).

2. Baptism of Fire

The baptism of fire is mentioned by John the Baptist in Matthew 3:11, but the context is crucial to understanding its meaning. This phrase was directed against the Pharisees and Sadducees who came to observe John baptizing believers in the Jordan River (Matthew 3:5-7). After warning in verse 10 that "every tree" that does not bear "good fruit" will be cut down and thrown into the fire, John makes a powerful statement: "I indeed baptize you with water unto repentance: but he that cometh after me is mightier than I, whose shoes I am not worthy to bear: he shall baptize you with the Holy Ghost, and with fire" (Matthew 3:11).

The baptism of the Holy Spirit refers to salvation, but what does it mean to be baptized with fire? The answer is found in the following verse: "Whose fan is in his (Christ's) hand, and he will thoroughly purge his floor, and gather his wheat into the garner; but he will burn up the chaff with unquenchable fire" (Matthew 3:12).

To those in the charismatic movement, this verse often represented speaking in tongues. They believed that once a person was baptized with the Holy Spirit, the immediate result was speaking in tongues. Hence, the baptism of the Holy Spirit and the baptism of fire were synonymous. However, according to John, this is far from the truth. John's train of thought remains unbroken from verse 10 through verse 12. He begins by addressing the hypocrisy and impending judgment of the Pharisees and Sadducees, and he concludes with the same theme. In summary, the baptism of fire represents "everlasting punishment"—the condemnation and wrath that the Lord will pronounce upon the wicked (Matthew 25:41, 46; Revelation 20:10, 14-15).

3. Born Again and Holy Spirit Baptism

Let's revisit the original question: "What does it mean to be 'born of the Spirit'?" The Apostle Peter provides some valuable insight into the concept of being born again:

"Being born again, not of corruptible seed, but of incorruptible, by the word of God, which liveth and abideth for ever" (1 Peter 1:23).

When we carefully examine this verse, the truth becomes evident. If we were to ask Peter how one is born again, he would answer, "By the word of God" (cf. Ephesians 6:17; 2

Timothy 3:16-17). Thus, being born again occurs when one applies the word of God, doing what God commands in the way He prescribes.

A common misconception within the charismatic movement is the inability to distinguish between Holy Spirit baptism and being born again. Holy Spirit baptism, as experienced by the apostles (Acts 2) and Cornelius (Acts 10; 11:1-18), bestowed miraculous gifts upon the recipients. In contrast, being born again is essential to salvation and has nothing to do with the miraculous.

Consider the example in the Gospel of Matthew, where a man could perform miracles yet was still lost. In Matthew 10, Jesus instructed His apostles:

"Go not into the way of the Gentiles, and any city of the Samaritans enter ye not: but go rather to the lost sheep of the house of Israel. And as ye go, preach, saying, the kingdom of heaven is at hand. Heal the sick, cleanse the lepers, raise the dead, cast out devils: freely ye have received, freely give" (Matthew 10:5-7, emphasis added, BM. Cf. vs 1).

These verses are called the Limited Commission (cf. Matthew 28:18-20, known as the Great Commission). Jesus was sending His apostles out to preach about the coming kingdom, and on this journey, they were endowed with the ability to perform various miracles.

Now, keeping this in mind, let's turn to Acts 10, where we find a man described as "a devout man, and one that feared God with all his house, which gave much alms to the people, and prayed to God always" (Acts 10:2). Despite his devoutness, this man, a Roman centurion named Cornelius, was lost. Around 3:00 P.M., Cornelius received a vision in which an angel instructed him to send for Simon, whose surname was Peter. This servant of Christ would tell Cornelius what he needed to do to attain salvation (Acts 10:6; 11:14).

When I was part of the charismatic movement, this chapter was often used as a proof text to argue that everyone should receive the baptism of the Holy Ghost. According to this interpretation, when Cornelius and his household received the miraculous measure of the Holy Spirit, they began to speak in tongues (Acts 10:46), and I falsely believed that these events occurred through the power of Cornelius's prayer (Acts 10:4). "What a story! What a testimony!" I thought. But I failed to grasp the small details that would dismantle the charismatic doctrine of Holy Spirit baptism.

For instance, the Bible states that Peter was going to speak "words" to Cornelius, and these "words" would reveal God's plan of salvation (Acts 11:14). Yet, when Cornelius received the Holy Spirit baptism, Peter had only "begun to speak" (Acts 11:15). This discrepancy troubled me. How could it be that God, through His servant, said that Cornelius's response to the word would save him, but before the word was even presented, the Holy Spirit fell on Cornelius and his household? Did God lie? Did Peter, God's anointed minister, add something to God's command? Was the angel misinformed? (Compare Luke's statement in Acts 10:44-46).

Thankfully, God does not leave us in the dark. Peter later clarified that the Holy Spirit did not fall on Cornelius and his household to save them. Instead, this event occurred to show all mankind that the Gentiles were to be accepted into the kingdom of God (Acts 11:17-18; 10:45). After this sign was given, Peter undoubtedly taught them the plan of salvation. Once they heard it, they were all baptized for the remission of sins (Acts 10:47-48). This group of Gentiles was born again by responding to God's word.

In conclusion, the story of Cornelius illustrates a clear distinction between Holy Spirit baptism and being born again. Being born again is brought about by one's response to God's word, while Holy Spirit baptism was a direct gift from God, separate from His word. Additionally, receiving the baptismal measure of the Holy Spirit had nothing to do with salvation; it was merely a sign to prove to the Jews that the Gentiles were to have access to the kingdom. On the other hand, being born again was, and still is, synonymous with salvation.

4. Baptism for the Dead

The third type of baptism we'll examine is baptism for the dead, as mentioned in 1 Corinthians 15:29. Some interpret this verse to suggest that a living person can be baptized on behalf of a deceased loved one. While this practice might have occurred during Paul's time, it is essential to note that Paul is not endorsing it. In the second century, heretical sects such as those led by Cerinthus and Marcion practiced baptism for the dead, yet the early church universally denounced this.

Additionally, it's crucial to observe that Paul uses the third-person pronoun in this verse. This suggests he was not speaking of himself or the brethren at Corinth. Instead, he was aware of this practice but did not condone it. Paul intended to caution the Christians in Corinth against the prevalent false practices surrounding them.

5. Water Baptism

The next type of baptism presented in the Bible is water baptism. The Scriptures discuss two distinct forms: the baptism of John and the Lord's baptism.

John's baptism involved water, as clearly demonstrated in the books of Matthew and John (Matthew 3:1-12; John 3:23). John's central message was that the kingdom "is at hand" (Matthew 3:2), indicating that his baptism occurred during the preparatory stage of the kingdom. Jesus Himself remarked:

"For I say unto you, among those that are born of women there is not a greater prophet than John the Baptist: but he that is least in the kingdom of God is greater than he" (Luke 7:28).

John's baptism was for the "remission of sins" (Mark 1:4; Luke 3:3). Understanding the purpose of baptism, John questioned Jesus, saying, "I have a need to be baptized of thee, and comest thou to me?" (Matthew 3:14). John recognized that Jesus was perfect and without sin. Water baptism would not remit any sins for a sinless man. However, Jesus stated that His reason for being baptized was to "fulfill all righteousness" (Matthew 3:15). As the perfect example in all things, Jesus demonstrated the necessity of baptism by being baptized.

Shortly after Jesus' resurrection, a new baptism was instituted, rendering John's baptism no longer valid. This is evident in the preaching of Apollos, who was "mighty in the Scriptures" (Acts 18:24), yet only knew of John's baptism (Acts 18:25). Aquila and Priscilla, two of Paul's Christian companions, explained to Apollos "the way of God more perfectly" (Acts 18:26). They taught him that the baptism of Jesus had superseded John's baptism. While it was still performed with water (Acts 2:38), it was now administered "in the name of the Father, and of the Son, and the Holy Ghost" (Matthew 28:19). This baptism symbolizes the Lord's death, burial, and resurrection (Romans 6:3-6), serves as the means of washing away one's sins (Acts 22:16), and enables one to put on Christ (Galatians 3:27).

To those within the charismatic movement, this doctrine may seem nonsensical. Many, like other denominational followers, view baptism as merely symbolic and believe it has no role in salvation. They treat the Holy Bible like a scrapbook, picking and choosing passages that align with their beliefs while overlooking those that challenge their doctrines. However, some within the charismatic group, particularly those with Pentecostal backgrounds or those who had strayed from the true church, believed in the necessity of baptism.

The leaders of the charismatic movement, however, often rejected water baptism. They tended to take straightforward passages and complicate them with mystical interpretations that only they claimed to understand. They added words and meanings that, according to them, could only be supplied by the Spirit. These leaders were revered almost as angelic figures, believed to be uniquely indwelt by the Spirit.

Speaking in Tongues

Speaking in tongues is a central focus of the charismatic movement. Adherents believe that it is the definitive sign of salvation. This belief is so strong that they consider speaking in tongues as essential evidence of one's true faith. During the first century, there was a diversity of spiritual gifts, but charismatics believed that all true believers should possess the ability to speak in tongues. They perceive it as the language of angels (1 Corinthians 13:1), a means of communicating with God in His tongue or delivering divine messages to others. Additionally, they view it as the Spirit making intercessions for the faithful, so speaking in tongues is often incorporated into their prayers. They base this belief on passages such as Romans 8:26 and Hebrews 5:11, interpreting these verses to mean that humans cannot pray to God correctly, so the Spirit inserts spiritual words that only God can understand.

New believers in the movement sometimes struggle with speaking in tongues. I, for example, needed assistance in the beginning. I was given written words to practice, meant to help me become more fluent in speaking in tongues—essentially "help aids" for the Holy Spirit.

However, charismatics often misunderstand the true nature of tongues as described in the New Testament. A simple study reveals that speaking in tongues involved known languages of that time (Acts 2:9-11). Furthermore, the ability to speak in tongues was just one of many gifts given by the Holy Spirit (1 Corinthians 12:7-10). In the following chapter, Paul explains that these spiritual gifts would eventually vanish. When? "When that which is perfect is come" (1 Corinthians 13:8-10). Later in this study, I will demonstrate that the "perfect" refers to the completed Word of God.

Demon Possession

One evening, while Peter was still on campus at Vincennes, a young man entered the classroom where we were gathered for Bible study. I remember his disheveled appearance: dark, greasy, long hair, a thin frame, and a pale complexion. He walked slowly and silently into the room, found a seat in the corner, and sat down. Once the young man was seated, Peter continued his speech. However, during the class, the young man grew increasingly agitated. After the class was over, Peter confronted this seemingly troubled individual. At that moment, something strange occurred.

Peter began to speak in tongues, and the young man responded kindly. Suddenly, Peter touched the young man's forehead, commanding the demon to leave his body. Before our eyes, it appeared as if a battle was unfolding between the forces of good and evil—or at least, that's what we believed at the time.

After a prolonged struggle, the young man collapsed to the floor. Wiping the sweat from his brow, Peter turned to his loyal followers and declared, "What you have witnessed is the power of God over the power of Satan." As the young man seemed to calm down, Peter informed us that he had cast out the demon. This declaration was met with cheers, as it wasn't every day that we witnessed such a dramatic event.

As time passed and I attended more Bible studies, I encountered many startling events. However, after witnessing a few of these so-called miraculous occurrences, I began to feel uneasy. It appears every vice a person had was attributed to demonic possession. One of my friends was dragged to the communion table in a local denomination because they believed he had a "demon of smoke" due to his addiction to cigarettes. Another was told he was possessed because of his weight, and yet another was exorcised for having a "demon of profanity." The list could go on and on.

However, the New Testament paints a different picture of demon possession than I was taught. In every New Testament example, the possessed individuals acted as though they were insane— "lunatic" is perhaps a better word. Yet my friends were not insane; they were intelligent people seeking an education at a reputable college. Their vices stemmed from human weakness, not demonic influence. It wasn't a demon that led them to do wrong; it was their lust. The book of James confirms this, stating:

> *Let no man say when he is tempted, I am tempted of God: for God cannot be tempted with evil, neither tempteth he any man: but every man is tempted, when he is drawn away of **his own lust**, and enticed* (Jas, 1:13, 14).

One may ask, "What about the man in Peter's class?" To this day, I have no answer to the identity of this college student. Several fellow students identified the man as being a Satan worshipper. Others engaged in the rumour that he practiced witchcraft. The truth is that **lies** are all a part of the charismatic movement. Thus, more than likely, it was all staged by Peter to build upon his ego.

The Second Coming

During my time in the charismatic movement, literature constantly circulated that claimed to reveal the many recognizable signs of Christ's second coming. Charismatics are often preoccupied with predicting the world's end, convinced that it is near. One tract even claimed that vultures in certain parts of the world were laying more eggs, supposedly preparing for Armageddon. Other tracts testified that ministers were raising the dead in far-off places like Africa and India.

One day, a friend of mine burst into my room, excitedly exclaiming, "Bill, you have to hear this tape!" When I asked what it was, he responded, "This one from David Wilkerson!"

David Wilkerson was a well-known Pentecostal minister who claimed to have received a vision from God. The "The Vision" tape profoundly impacted charismatic believers across America. As I sat on my bed listening to every word, people from the hallway were drawn into my room, captivated by the powerful voice that filled the space. By the time the tape ended, nine or ten people had gathered to hear the harrowing message that poured from my tape machine.

Wilkerson's vision depicted the coming of the Antichrist, the arrival of God's kingdom, and the second coming of Christ.

His portrayal of these events sent chills down my spine. I had never heard anyone speak with such simplicity and sincerity. Every word seemed to come from the heart, and I felt like I had listened to a prophet.

However, if one were to count the number of times these so-called prophets have been wrong, it would dissuade anyone from following such charismatic leaders. Someone is always new, proclaiming this or that about the second-coming events, yet they consistently misinterpret one section or another from the Book of Revelation.

The bulk of charismatic doctrine is rooted in the book of Revelation. They focus on the book's vivid imagery and interpret it literally, using this as the foundation upon which they build their beliefs.

Yet, Jesus Himself, speaking about His return, said, "But of that day and hour knoweth no man, no, not the angels of heaven, but my Father only" (Matthew 24:36). Mark also records Jesus saying, "But of that day and that hour knoweth no man, no, not the angels which are in heaven, neither the Son, but the Father" (Mark 13:32). If the Lord declares that He does not know the time of His return, how can the charismatic claim to? The only way such testimonies can be accepted or taught is by distorting God's sacred message, a skill the charismatic disciple sadly excels at.

A Demon Story

It was a cold winter in 1974. We traveled a short distance from campus to a small trailer where a Bible study would be held. A young couple, both deeply involved in the charismatic movement, lived in that trailer. That night, they wanted to share a terrifying story they believed to be accurate.

The man began by recounting that, several nights ago, he and his wife were home alone when they heard what they described as a faint voice coming from the bathroom. At first, they thought it was just the wind. However, even after the wind subsided, the voice persisted. The man then explained that he cautiously made his way to the bathroom. When he opened the door, he saw nothing. But as he stepped inside and looked into the mirror, he screamed. His wife rushed in to find her husband curled up in the fetal position on the floor. As he whimpered in her arms, he claimed that there was a demon in the mirror speaking to him.

"What did the demon say?" his wife asked. "He wanted me!" the husband replied.

After he calmed down, the couple knelt in prayer. They claimed to have prayed for hours, and when they finally stood up, they felt specific in their hearts that the demon had left. They cried out, "Praise God," proclaiming victory in Jesus. There was no doubt in their minds that the apparition was actual. What the man perceived in that mirror was as accurate to him as the wife who came to his rescue.

After the couple shared their story, everyone who heard it was horrified. If I had any doubts about my charismatic faith, this story dispelled them. It convinced me that miracles still existed and that Satan and his demons could still possess the souls of men. But then, I later came across the words of Paul:

"...even him, whose coming is after the working of Satan with all power and signs and lying wonders, and with all deceivableness of unrighteousness in them that perish; because they received not the love of the truth, that they might be saved. And for this cause, God shall send them strong delusion, that they should believe a lie: that they all might be damned who believed not the truth but had pleasure in unrighteousness" (2 Thessalonians 2:9-12).

Years later, I realized this couple experienced a "strong delusion." They had rejected the proper way of God, and because of their unwavering commitment to the philosophies of the movement, they believed what they envisioned to be true. However, God does not lie. The Bible reveals that such things no longer occur (1 Corinthians 13:10; James 1:25; Acts 8:18). It should be evident how deceptive our minds can be. Today, many are not possessed by demons but by the monsters that dwell within the confines of their minds.

The Gift of Prophecy

I recall a moment during a Bible study that impacted my faith journey. We had gathered as usual, delving into the Scriptures and enjoying one another's fellowship. Suddenly, the atmosphere shifted with the entrance of a woman who claimed to possess the gift of prophecy. To those who embrace Pentecostal beliefs, this gift can manifest in two ways: predicting future events or revealing the hidden aspects of one's spirit.

The tranquil Bible study was disrupted that evening when this woman stood up and announced that she had received a divine revelation. She claimed God was displeased with a particular individual in our midst. Instantly, a wave of tension swept through the group. Whispers and uneasy glances followed each person, wondering who among us might be the subject of her revelation.

She continued, revealing that the person in question was a male, narrowing down the potential candidates. Eventually, a young student bravely confessed that he had been struggling with lustful thoughts. The room's reaction was a mix of shock and relief. "Praise God!" one of our enthusiastic members exclaimed, while another declared, "God has revealed this to you!"

The prophetic woman then laid hands on the young man, praying fervently for the deliverance from the temptation he faced. This act, though well-intentioned, seemed to shift the dynamic of our Bible studies. The sessions became fraught with anxiety as the fear of personal sins being exposed grew among us. The group's unity faltered, and we eventually moved our meetings elsewhere.

Reflecting on this experience, I now see how my understanding of prophecy and spiritual gifts was limited. I lacked the depth of knowledge found in passages like 1 Corinthians 13:10 and James 1:25, which speak to the cessation of sure miraculous gifts and the enduring power of Scripture. In those days, I believed that miracles, tongues, and prophecies were ongoing, and questioning them felt like asking God Himself.

Looking back, I regret not dedicating more time to studying the Bible and deepening my faith. Although my academic record was modest, my approach to Scripture was even less disciplined. Yet, this period of struggle and misunderstanding became a catalyst for growth. It reminded me of the importance of grounding our faith in a well-rounded knowledge of the Word and trusting in its guidance above all else.

The Role of Women and the Nature of Healing

In my journey through the charismatic movement, I understood the significant role women played in this sphere. They were actively involved in preaching, serving, and sharing their testimonies, often disregarding the instructions found in 1

Timothy 2:11-14, which suggests that women should not exercise authority over men and should remain silent.

I once confronted a firm believer in Pentecostal teachings about this issue. His response was puzzling: "It's not the women who are in control, but the Holy Spirit speaking through them." This answer left me baffled and led me to question further. "What does 'remain silent' mean, then?" I asked. The response was delayed and non-existent, leaving me to ponder the definition of silence in the context of this discussion. I encountered similar evasions when discussing the matter with a woman preacher.

The challenge with the charismatic movement lies in its selective interpretation of Scripture. Believers often decide which verses are literal and which are figurative based on their experiences and beliefs, leading to widespread misunderstanding. This selective approach can undermine a deep, comprehensive understanding of the Bible, making many reliant on charismatic leaders for their religious convictions.

The distinction between women in the charismatic movement and those in traditional Pentecostal circles is noteworthy. Charismatic women often exhibit a liberal style, embracing modern fashion and personal adornments, unlike their Pentecostal counterparts, who adhere to stricter dress codes and avoid makeup and jewelry. Over time, some of these traditional restrictions have evolved, reflecting broader cultural shifts within many denominations.

While the charismatic movement shares some beliefs with Pentecostalism, it primarily revolves around the conviction of the Holy Spirit's presence and its manifestations, including speaking in tongues and receiving visions.

The Nature of Spiritual Healing

It doesn't take long in the charismatic movement to encounter claims of divine healing. I recall a young man who spoke of a miraculous recovery from a brain tumor. Despite ongoing medical treatments, the tumor reportedly vanished after fervent prayer. Similarly, many healings were attributed to the laying on of hands by leaders, and when healing didn't occur, it was often attributed to the individual's lack of faith.

One significant experience from my younger years involved a tragic event where a friend, a Chinese Buddhist monk, suffered a severe accident. Despite our collective prayers for his recovery, he passed away. This loss challenged my understanding of healing and faith.

During Jesus' ministry, healing often occurred instantaneously. Lazarus was raised from the dead, and the blind man received sight immediately, without gradual healing. Miracles, as described in the New Testament, happened instantaneously and wholly, contrasting with modern claims of gradual or partial healing.

Furthermore, Jesus' miracles were public and widely recognized, drawing significant attention. If true miracles were happening today, they would undoubtedly be reported widely and cannot be concealed. Many contemporary faith healers have been exposed as fraudulent, yet they continue to attract support.

The cases of prominent figures like Oral Roberts and Jimmy Swaggart, who have faced public scandals while claiming miraculous powers, highlight the need for discernment. Despite their failings, these individuals continued to attract followers and financial support, raising questions about their ministries' true nature.

I urge those supporting such figures to seek clarity in Scripture rather than the spectacle of modern faith healing. The churches of Christ remain steadfast in their commitment to God's Word, emphasizing faith rooted in Scripture rather than miraculous signs. Our belief is anchored not in the need to see miracles but in the enduring truth of God's Word (Rom. 10:17). This reliance on Scripture over sensationalism is a testament to the strength of faith that does not require physical evidence to believe.

The Spirit Reveals

During my visits to the Lord's church in Vincennes, Indiana, I experienced a profound sense of community and warmth. Dr. Nelson, a faculty member at Vincennes University, was incredibly impactful with his kindness and strong spirit. Through his example, the path back to God began to illuminate before me.

I remember a pivotal moment when a fellow charismatic and I attended services at Vincennes. The minister's teachings on baptism sparked controversy. My friend was adamant about not needing baptism because he had the Spirit. He argued that his spiritual experiences rendered water baptism unnecessary. Despite knowing in my heart that baptism was integral to salvation, I chose to support my friend rather than confront the truth.

This choice haunted me for years. It was a painful realization that I had compromised my understanding of Christ's doctrine to maintain harmony within our group. Often, we find ourselves sacrificing our spiritual convictions to fit in with others, whether for familial loyalty, group acceptance, or denominational allegiance. No commitment should ever outweigh the importance of our soul's salvation.

My friend's confusion about baptism highlighted the broader issue: how easily human emotions and loyalties can obscure clear biblical teachings. It's a reminder of the importance of standing firm in the truth, even when it challenges our relationships or comfort zones.

The Music Ministry

I deeply immersed myself in the vibrant, emotional atmosphere of charismatic worship. Our Bible study sessions were lively, with guitars strummed and voices raised in ecstatic praise. Music became the heartbeat of our gatherings, creating an intense emotional experience that seemed to define our worship.

The confusion in charismatic worship was often palpable. Despite the enthusiasm and energy, our sessions frequently left us no closer to understanding the true essence of worship. The focus on musical elements—guitars, drums, and other instruments—shifted attention away from the Creator and the experience itself.

I have observed a shift in the Lord's church today. Acapella groups now take the stage, record albums, and receive acclaim. While their talent is undeniable, the focus on performance and entertainment can overshadow the true purpose of worship: to glorify God, not to showcase human skill.

The Ichthus Music Festival in Wilmore, Kentucky, was a prime example of this trend. Modeled as a religious counterpart to Woodstock, it aimed to inspire people to be "high on Jesus" rather than drugs. Yet, many attendees seemed to meld Jesus into a reflection of their desires rather than encountering Him as He is.

The emotional highs experienced in charismatic worship can be addicting. Music becomes a drug, providing a temporary spiritual boost but leaving one craving more. When the music fades, the emptiness can be profound, revealing a dependence on the emotional aspects of worship rather than its actual substance.

Returning home for the summer, I found myself struggling with depression. The absence of the group and the music left me feeling lost, and I dismissed my parents' traditional church practices as ignorant. I questioned how worship could be meaningful without the instruments and vitality that had become so central to my experience.

However, truth has a way of persisting. Despite my resistance, the echoes of God's word haunted my thoughts, revealing deeper realities about worship and faith. Proverbs 23:23 reminds us to "Buy the truth and sell it not." Even when I resisted, the truth remained, guiding me to a more profound understanding of worship grounded in God's Word rather than emotional experiences.

Testimonies

Throughout my time in the charismatic movement, I was frequently exposed to the stories of individuals who claimed to have been transformed by Jesus. These testimonies often came from those who had previously struggled with addiction or lived troubled lives, sharing how their encounters with Christ had changed them. While the transformation they described was fundamental, it became clear that the truth of Scripture did not always change their lives.

A memorable instance was in the 1970s when my brother, a friend, and I traveled to Warsaw, Indiana, to hear Nicky Cruz. Cruz, famously converted from gang life by David Wilkerson, was the subject of the book and film *The Cross and the Switchblade*. The event drew thousands eager to hear Cruz's powerful testimony. His dramatic delivery and past struggles resonated with many, symbolizing hope and redemption for those present.

Charismatic circles often see such figures as heroes—living proof of God's transformative power. The stories of their pasts serve as motivational examples, encouraging others to believe they, too, can change. However, I began to see these events as "Testimonies for a Buck." They often focused more on fundraising and emotional appeal than on delivering sound doctrine. The pressure to give generously and the glamorization of the speakers highlighted a troubling trend: the presentation of personal stories as gospel truth without substantive doctrinal teaching.

Emotional displays in worship can be genuine and moving, and I've seen sincere believers express sincere feelings during prayer. Yet, many charismatic ministers appeared to manipulate emotions, turning them on and off like a faucet. This was especially apparent in events like the one in Warsaw.

That night, he had lasting repercussions. My brother, initially raised in the Lord's church, was influenced by the charismatic philosophy he encountered. He began to question his known teachings and shifted toward a more liberal understanding of faith. Despite my efforts to guide him back to the truth, he remains distanced from the core doctrines I hold dear.

The experience underscored a dangerous compromise: the belief that multiple interpretations of faith are acceptable. Such a view, based on human reasoning rather than divine revelation, offers a false sense of security. I have come to understand that true security rests solely in Christ and His teachings.

The growth and success of denominations compared to the perceived stagnation of the Lord's church often leads to disillusionment. Denominational leaders may preach to satisfy "itching ears," compromising doctrine for numerical growth and emotional appeal. This approach can lead to a superficial faith that lacks true substance.

Having experienced denominationalism's shortcomings and its diluted gospel, I returned to a deeper commitment to God's truth. The pursuit of sound doctrine and authentic worship remains my focus, especially as I witness others within the church veer toward teachings that prioritize human desires over divine truth.

XIII. A Time to Fast

Fasting was a challenging practice for me during my early years in the charismatic movement. Unlike the approach Jesus described in Matthew 6:17-18, where fasting is a private matter between the individual and God, the charismatics often imposed fasting practices on their followers. Fasts were scheduled and breaking them could lead to condemnation from the group.

My experience with wrestling, where strict dieting was required, made the enforced fasting even more difficult. Although I understood the importance of fasting and recognized its value, how it was handled within the charismatic community felt oppressive. I found myself struggling with the control exerted over me despite my willingness to fast for personal and spiritual growth.

Jesus did speak about fasting, particularly in the context of faith and spiritual power (Matthew 17:20-21), but He did not prescribe specific times or methods. According to Jesus, fasting should be a private and personal discipline associated with prayer and humility. It was meant to be a voluntary act, not something mandated by others.

During these fasting periods, I resorted to small acts of deception, like buying a candy bar to quell my hunger momentarily. While it was a temporary relief, it also highlighted the disconnect between the spirit of fasting and how it was practiced in that environment.

XIV. Serving Brother Billy

During my time at Vincennes University, my group had the chance to participate in an event related to Billy Graham's movie, *A Time to Run*. Despite being Baptist and our group being charismatic, Graham welcomed our involvement in providing counselors for those responding to the movie's invitation.

At the event, we were given name tags and booklets to help guide people who came forward. I took several individuals aside and used the booklet to teach them about salvation. However, I soon noticed that different counselors, including some of my own comrades, were mixing in their philosophies. Graham's omission of the baptism of the Holy Spirit led to various doctrines being presented to the seekers.

This experience highlighted the problematic nature of denominationalism. Despite the surface-level cooperation, the differences in doctrine revealed the divisions within Christianity. Although we charismatics saw ourselves as having a special connection with God, the lack of uniformity in teachings demonstrated that we were not all on the same path to salvation.

The incident underscored the issue of compromising fundamental truths for group cohesion and friendship. In my desire to fit in and maintain relationships, I had sacrificed essential aspects of the faith, revealing the limitations of denominational cooperation regarding core doctrines.

I. A Few Things Learned

The charismatic community teaches many false doctrines, but there are also some things we can learn from them. For example, in my ten years of being charismatic, I knew that giving was not difficult. Although I complained about all the unique offerings, I never had a problem giving. Whether it was my time, money, or whatever, giving became enjoyable. The more I gave, the better I felt.

Giving is something they don't speak about among many of my brethren in the Lord's church. For them, giving is a burden. This ought not to be so! We belong to God and should make the denominational world look bad. We are the examples, not them. In many situations, pressure is used to get people to give, or gimmicks are employed to entice funds from the so-called faithful. These gimmicks range from selling holy water to advertising books and tapes. Whatever the case may be, the charismatic learns early to give generously.

Their giving was also focused on the group's survival. Without funds, the message would not reach beyond the block. Tracts, Bibles, and other necessities were not bought with good looks. The excuse, "I'm sending my money to some charity group," was not tolerated. If one wanted to send a little, that was fine, but the bulk of one's giving had better be centered in the movement.

We, who claim to be the actual people of God, need to conquer these negative attitudes toward giving. Are you the kind of person who gives five dollars to the local congregation and then sends the rest elsewhere? Are you the kind of person who gives and then takes back what is God's? I have seen many Christians get upset with certain decisions made by elders and then lower their contributions. My brethren, these things ought not to be.

The local congregation is the most essential feature of any town or city. We are the messengers of God, charged with preaching the gospel to the world. Without funds, buildings will deteriorate, and congregations will fold. It is sad to say, but many will not attend services if the church gathers in someone's home. Most religious people have come to believe that the church is the building. Although this is the wrong philosophy, having a local gathering place where the saints can meet is friendly.

Another aspect central to the charismatic philosophy is prayer. I found myself praying all the time when I was active in the charismatic movement. I would pray during class and after class. I thanked God for the grades I received, my teachers, and the dormitory room I slept in. There wasn't anything I was not thankful for, and I gave all the praise and glory to God.

Every true charismatic believes in the power of prayer. If they prayed over someone sick and that person was not healed, it was because that person did not have enough faith. They knew this because one firmly came to believe that God was listening. Little did I realize that my prayers were not going further than the top of my dormitory ceiling. Just a brief study of the story of the raising of Lazarus proved that it didn't take faith for someone to be healed. After all, how much faith did Lazarus have, being dead? (John 11).

We who are in the kingdom need to understand the power of prayer. These people who believed things contrary to the word of God prayed without ceasing. Every chance they got, they bowed before God, believing that He was attentive to every word spoken. Yet, many of us who are true disciples of Christ find ourselves too busy to kneel in prayer, and when we do, our prayers are short and sweet. We need to comprehend the true meaning of being dependent on God. The privilege of communicating with Him should motivate us to speak to Him as often as we can. After all, prayer is a privilege.

Prayer for the sick should be offered before the throne of God. Though we may not believe in miracles today, the providence of God is still a reality. "What is the providence of God?" one may ask. It is simply God's active participation in one's life. You may not be able to prove it one way or the other, but it still does not negate the hand of God in the affairs of men.

A miracle, if you remember from our previous discussion, was undeniable. A blind man healed instantly is beyond the realm of human comprehension. A dead man being raised was an act that proved the power of Christ, and once again, the evidence was too clear to deny.

Yet, when someone is dying, and prayers are offered on their behalf, and then after a while, they begin to recover, some proclaim this to be a miracle. The problem is a recovery such as this does not fit the Biblical definition of a miracle. Jesus would speak, and the healing would take place instantly. Not only that, but the masses in the first century were healed completely. The blind men could see; the dead could walk, and the lepers were cleansed of their leprosy.

Today, we have, on many occasions, prayed for our sick. Sometimes, a person diagnosed with a terminal disease turns for the better and gets well. The doctors usually have their prognosis, whereas many of us believe it was the power of God's hands that caused them to get better. For me, to prove this would be impossible. Therefore, I term this "the providence of God." Later in this book, an entire section is dedicated to this topic. Thus, this is something to ponder.

Another positive aspect of the charismatic movement was its energy to evangelize. Young charismatics found themselves sharing the charismatic message with every person they met. It became a way of life. At first, the young charismatics might be nervous when sharing their testimony with someone, but after a short period, the tension leaves, and one begins to feel convicted when not sharing.

The devil wants us to sit back and do nothing. He realizes that many cults and movements are out there preaching doctrines contrary to the Word. Procrastination is the devil's trademark in the heart of believers, but for every second we sit idle, someone with a false conviction is teaching our neighbors and friends.

The charismatic movement was also a very close-knit group. I appreciate the concept that every person is essential. This is undoubtedly the actual concept of the Lord's church. However, when we find this more so in the denominational world, there must be a problem. Preachers scream out for members to draw closer to one another. We find cliques forming and congregations growing apart. Once again, this should not be happening in the Lord's church. I encourage every reader of this book to draw close to every church member. Get to know your brothers and sisters. Find out their needs. Usually, the people we so quickly dislike are those individuals we never took the time to know. People remark, "I have nothing in common with that person," but usually, they do not know the person they are wary of. The Bible says concerning the converts on Pentecost, "And all that believed were together, and had all things common" (Acts 2:44). I don't believe this verse teaches that all these people liked the same foods, enjoyed the same entertainment, and dressed the same way. No, these people had "all things common," spiritually speaking. Their link was Christ. They enjoyed discussing and studying about Jesus. They shared in the same joy, knowing His blood saved them. So, they had much to talk about, and most of all, they felt the power of unity. They were united in Christ; thus, "they had all things in common."

CONVERTING THE CHARISMATIC

Undoubtedly, if we were to gather fifty Christians and ask them how to evangelize the world, we would likely get fifty different responses. Therefore, my insight on how to convert the charismatic comes from my personal experience. Having been a charismatic for ten years should lend some weight to my reasoning.

The Power of Love

The first step in converting the charismatic is through LOVE! Although this should be a term familiar to every church member, it often isn't. The charismatic individual is surrounded by a community that offers protective love. This characteristic of the movement makes it particularly appealing to young people.

When approaching a firm believer in the charismatic movement, they must perceive the same love from us. If we come on too strong or appear confused, they will use this against us, potentially burning the bridge we tried to build.

The Necessity of Patience

Secondly, one must have PATIENCE with the false believer. Solomon wisely stated, "Better is the end of a thing than the beginning thereof: and the patient in spirit is better than the proud in spirit" (Eccl. 7:8).

Patience is challenging. We humans often desire immediate results. The charismatic movement's individuals have been conditioned to believe certain things over many years. They have felt with their hearts and bringing them out of this world of false teaching may take time.

Controlling One's Temper

In addition to patience and love, one must CONTROL their TEMPER. I recall being evangelized by my brothers and sisters in the Church of Christ. My responses to their comments often triggered anger, destroying all their efforts. It was akin to wrestling, where making the opponent angry would lead to their defeat.

To convert someone, one must remain in control. The charismatic may try to provoke negative emotions to undermine the conversation. Remaining calm and composed is crucial to preventing these efforts from derailing the discussion.

Understanding the Driver's Seat

Another essential aspect of evangelizing the charismatic is the concept of the driver's SEAT. I once lived in a house surrounded by an iron fence. One day, as I was leaving, I realized I had left the keys inside. While I ran in to get them, my young child Billy, who was barely one and a half, managed to put the truck in motion and crash it into the gate.

This incident taught me two lessons: I underestimated the child's abilities, and children shouldn't be behind the wheel. Similarly, we may underestimate the charismatic's knowledge. Many are well-versed in Scripture and can converse logically about the Bible. Therefore, DON'T UNDERESTIMATE THE CHARISMATIC.

Preparation and Common Ground

Before refuting a well-versed charismatic, one must thoroughly know the Word of God. If one is not prepared, chaos will ensue. It is crucial to understand the opposition. Learn about their beliefs, study diligently, and avoid presumptions. Failure to do so will hinder the effort to convert them.

Start with the points of doctrine that you have in COMMON with your opponent. Avoid attacking their false doctrines immediately, as this will create a defensive barrier. Instead, begin with areas of agreement. The communication bridge will evolve through several discussions on common ground, allowing you to address and correct their misconceptions gradually.

By employing love, patience, temperance, and thorough preparation, we can engage effectively with charismatic individuals and guide them toward the truth.

Undoubtedly, if we were to gather fifty Christians and ask them how to evangelize the world, we would likely get fifty different responses. Therefore, my insight on how to convert the charismatic comes from my personal experience. Having been a charismatic for ten years should lend some weight to my reasoning.

The Power of Love

The first step in converting the charismatic is through LOVE! Although this should be a term familiar to every church member, it often isn't. The charismatic individual is surrounded by a community that offers protective love. This characteristic of the movement makes it particularly appealing to young people.

When approaching a firm believer in the charismatic movement, they must perceive the same love from us. If we come on too strong or appear confused, they will use this against us, potentially burning the bridge we tried to build.

Secondly, one must have PATIENCE with the false believer. Solomon wisely stated, "Better is the end of a thing than the beginning thereof: and the patient in spirit is better than the proud in spirit" (Eccl. 7:8).

Patience is challenging. We humans often desire immediate results. The charismatic movement's individuals have been conditioned to believe certain things over many years. They have felt it with their hearts, and bringing them out of this world of false teaching may take time.

There are several points of commonality between Christians and charismatics. For instance, charismatics believe that Jesus is Lord and emphasize that Jesus is God. They do not deny the Trinity (the Godhead) and accept the core elements of salvation—belief, repentance, and confession. However, it's essential to address the groups that adhere to the "Jesus Only" doctrine, which asserts that Jesus is the sole person in the Godhead. This belief is relatively easy to refute but requires careful preparation to debate effectively.

Interpreting the Bible

Charismatics generally view the Bible as inspired by the Holy Spirit. They believe that because the Bible is Spirit-inspired, one needs the Holy Spirit to interpret it accurately. This belief underscores the importance of understanding their perspective on scriptural interpretation and being prepared to address it thoughtfully.

Gradual Teaching

It is crucial to teach charismatics incrementally. Avoid overwhelming them with too many passages at once, leading to confusion. Instead, present one or two passages at a time, encourage them to study them independently, and then discuss them in detail. Just as infants are fed small amounts, new learners should be given digestible information.

One-on-One Evangelism

One-on-one evangelism is vital for effective conversion. Engaging charisma within a group setting can lead to mockery and confusion, making it challenging to convey the message. When evangelizing individually, you can address questions and concerns more directly, creating a more conducive environment for discussion.

Engaging with Spiritual Leaders

Eventually, you may encounter a charismatic, spiritual leader. It's crucial to be well-prepared for these discussions to influence the charismatic's beliefs. Keep control of the conversation and focus on evangelizing the soul rather than merely winning an argument. Charismatic leaders are adept at steering conversations, so it's essential to maintain composure and direct the discussion with care.

Maintaining Respect and Communication

Respect for the charismatic leader is essential. While they may be a false teacher, showing respect and avoiding aggressive tactics will prevent unnecessary conflicts. Your aim should be to open lines of communication rather than to confront or condemn.

Lessons from Experience

Reflecting on personal experiences can offer valuable lessons. For example, when my child witnessed me shoot a sick rabbit, it inadvertently caused emotional distress. This experience underscored the importance of thoughtful actions and consideration of their impact on others.

Always keep the lines of communication open. If discussions become heated, pausing and maintaining a friendly relationship is better. By keeping communication channels open, there's always a chance to influence someone positively.

In Luke 19:2-8, Jesus dined with publicans and sinners, demonstrating His care for their souls. Similarly, approaching charismatics with genuine care and respect can help convey the truth effectively. Even if it takes time and effort, some charismatics may eventually question their teachings and become open to the truth.

THE CHARISMATIC DOCTRINE REFUTED

This section addresses some of the key doctrines held by charismatics, particularly those I encountered during my ten years within the movement. It examines several major doctrinal points and their refutations.

"Jesus Only" Doctrine

The "Jesus Only" doctrine, particularly prevalent in the United Pentecostal Church, asserts that there is only one person in the Godhead: Jesus Christ. Proponents cite passages like Isaiah 44:24 and 1 Timothy 2:5, which emphasize God's singularity. However, these passages do not exclude the existence of multiple persons within the Godhead but rather highlight God's unity and singular authority.

Refutation:

Matthew 3:16-17 provides a clear visual representation of the Godhead. Jesus is baptized, the Spirit descends like a dove, and a voice from heaven declares Jesus as the Son. This manifestation cannot be explained as merely internal thoughts or illusions but demonstrates the distinct persons within the Godhead.

1 Corinthians 11:3 further supports the existence of multiple persons within the Godhead by stating that "the head of Christ is God." This indicates a hierarchical relationship, implying that Christ and God are distinct persons.

Baptism and the Holy Spirit

Charismatics often differentiate between two types of baptism: water baptism and Holy Spirit baptism. They refer to

Acts 2:38, Joel 2:28-31, and Acts 2:17-21, interpreting the "promise" in Acts 2:39 as referring to the Holy Spirit baptism.

Refutation:

Acts 2:38 refers to water baptism for the remission of sins and receiving the gift of the Holy Spirit. The promise of Holy Spirit baptism, however, was primarily for the apostles and not for all believers. Acts 1:4-8 and 1:11 indicate that the apostles were the primary recipients of the full measure of the Holy Spirit.

The event involving Cornelius (Acts 10) illustrates that the Holy Spirit's descent upon him and his household was a sign to the Jewish believers that the Gentiles were also to be included in God's plan, not a standard for all believers.

Acts 8:14-18 further clarifies that the apostles' miraculous gifts of the Spirit were imparted by the laying on of hands, not by the baptism of the Holy Spirit experienced by the apostles. This distinction highlights that miraculous gifts were not universally available to all believers.

Miracles and Their Purpose

Charismatics often view miracles as ongoing manifestations of the Holy Spirit's work. They believe that miracles continue today, similar to those in the early church.

Refutation:

Miracles in the first century were signs validating Christ's divine authority (John 20:30-31). Acts 8:12-18 shows that despite many conversions and baptisms, the miraculous gifts of the Spirit were only given through the apostles. This indicates that the widespread practice of miracles was limited to the apostolic era and not intended to continue indefinitely.

Apostles vs. Disciples

There is a distinction between apostles and disciples. Apostles were chosen to bear witness to the resurrection of Christ and had specific qualifications, including being with Jesus during His ministry and witnessing His resurrection (Acts 1:21-26).

Refutation:

This distinction underscores that the apostolic role and its accompanying miraculous gifts were unique to that period. The qualifications for apostleship and their specific role in the early church highlight that such roles and gifts were not intended for all believers but were foundational for establishing the church.

In summary, understanding and addressing these doctrinal points with careful scriptural analysis helps refute the charismatic teachings and clarify the biblical perspective.

FOOT WASHING

Another doctrine firmly believed by those who proclaim themselves to be charismatic is foot washing. The example is found in John 13:1-17. They focus on the verse that reads, *"For I have given you an example, that ye should do as I have done to you"* (Jn. 13:15).

The first time this happened to me was in my beginning days as a charismatic. Several of us had gathered. In the middle of the floor was a large container filled with water. We were asked to take off our shoes and socks. At this point, one by one, we stepped into the water-filled container, and the person in front of us would begin washing ours after he had his feet washed. At first, I was uneasy about the whole situation, but it became easier to accept after a period.

To the true charismatic, this example was binding. The Lord said to do it. Therefore, one had to obey. The Lord did not specify the number of times this was to be done. Hence, it was up to the spiritual leader to decide how often this would be performed. The problem with this doctrine is that it was not meant to be doctrine. In other words, charismatics focus on the act, not the lesson to be learned. During the days of our Lord's ministry, men and women wore sandals. It was typical that when one entered the home of another, he or she would wash his feet before entering. This way, one could wash off the dust accumulated from the natural surroundings.

What Jesus was trying to teach was servitude. *"Verily, verily, I say unto you, the servant is not greater than his lord; neither he that is sent greater than he that sent him"* (Jn. 13:16). They were being taught to serve one another. It was a lesson that they greatly needed. For the Lord knew that if the group could draw close together and serve one another, they would have the ability to spread the word to every corner of the globe.

The Lord wanted His apostles to learn the meaning of servitude and not to go out and teach foot washing as a part of Christian worship. A close look at the New Testament unveils that this was the only time the act of foot washing was administered. There are no other examples.

TONGUE SPEAKING

Another important doctrine believed by the charismatic community was tongue-speaking. Tongue speaking was that outward sign to prove that one had received the Holy Spirit. Without it, one would have no proof that he was saved. Their philosophy about tongue speaking rests in 1 Corinthians, chapter 12-14. Paul proclaimed, "*But the manifestation of the Spirit is given to every man to profit withal*" (1 Cor. 12:7). Thus, they believe this verse implies that the gifts were meant for every generation.

They also enforce the concept that tongue speaking is not any known language today. They quote Romans 8:26, "*Likewise the Spirit also helpeth our infirmities: for we know not what we should pray for as we ought: but the Spirit itself maketh intercession for us with groanings which cannot be uttered.*"

They will summarize their perspective by quoting First Corinthians chapter thirteen and verse one. Here, Paul speaks of the *"tongues of men and angels."*

In chapter fourteen, Paul declares that tongue-speaking is an *"unknown tongue"* (1 Cor. 14:2). Therefore, they conclude that this is a divine language that needs a Holy Spirit-filled interpreter, and without this person, tongue-speaking is but a prayer that the Holy Spirit is uttering through you.

The Charismatic faces several problems with his or her belief about tongue speaking. First, the gift of tongues was a gift of known languages. When the people who gathered on the day of Pentecost heard the apostles speak in tongues, the masses concluded, *"And how hear we every man in our* ***TONGUE, WHEREIN WE WERE BORN?"*** (Acts 2:8). Then in verses nine through eleven the different dialects are stated. From the very beginning when tongue speaking was introduced, the Bible identifies the gift of tongues to be the known languages of that day.

Also, if you have ever been to a charismatic worship service, one thing is notable- CONFUSION! You may have one person beside you speaking in tongues, another yelling at the top of his lungs, and the preacher with his microphone in hand, screaming for the responses from the crowd. If you are not participating in some way, you will surely be intimidated to get involved.

This is not what you read about in the first century church. Paul, to the Corinthian brethren wrote, *"Let all things be done decently and in order"* (1 Cor. 14:40). This is far from the typical worship service held in most charismatic settings in which I was involved. Paul would have surely felt out of place and ashamed of the events that happened at one of these meetings.

Secondly, in the first century church if one did speak in an unknown tongue there was also to be an interpreter present (1 Cor. 14:27). Notice what the next verse says, *"But if there be no interpreter, let him keep silence in the church; and let him speak of himself, and to God"* (1 Cor. 14:28). Occasionally you would find a person interpreting what one of the members was supposedly saying, but not often. In a worship setting there could be twenty or thirty people speaking in tongues at the same time. Common sense alone tells us that this was not acceptable in the sight of God.

Within the writings of Paul in First Corinthians chapter twelve through fourteen, an amazing prophesy unfolds. Paul declares, *"Charity never faileth: but whether there be prophecies, they shall fail; whether there be tongues, they shall cease; whether there be knowledge, it shall vanish away. For we know in part, and we prophesy in part. But when that which is perfect is come, then that which is in part shall be done away"* (1 Cor. 13:8-10).

Paul proclaims that when "*that which is perfect*" would come, the miracles would cease. The question is, "What is the THAT?" To many charismatics the "that" represents the second coming of Christ. When Jesus comes again there will be no need for miracles; therefore, they will cease. The problem with this view is the gender of the pronoun so used by Paul. "That" is neuter gender. Would you dare pray to Jesus and call Him an "it" or a "that?" Surely not! Whenever I pray, I use the masculine gender for Christ.

So, then, what is this "perfect" thing that would come and eliminate the need for miracles? The answer is given in the Bible. It has already been proven that the miraculous measure of the Holy Spirit could only be transmitted by the laying on of the apostles' hands, and when the last apostle died, the gift could no longer be transferred to others. Thus, when the last person who received the laying on of the apostles' hands passed away, the miracles vanished.

The book of James further states, "*But whoso looketh into the PERFECT law of liberty, and continueth therein, he being not a forgetful hearer, but a doer of the work, this man shall be blessed in his deed*" (Jas. 1:25).

James is talking about the word of God. His writing on the subject further supports what has previously been stated. Once the last inspired person died, there could no longer be anything added to the New Testament. Therefore, the New Testament

70

would be complete, and once it was completed, there would be no need for miracles to exist (cf. Jude 3 and Eph. 4:11-13).

BEWARE LEST YE FALL

Accumulating knowledge is a part of human existence. When we fail to do what is right before God, we get our just reward. This part of the narrative concentrates on why many of our brethren turn away from the truth and why it is necessary to feed our young people with the nourishment that comes from the Holy Bible.

First, let me point out that we sometimes fail initially. We feel that if we teach them the basics, just enough to get them in the water, that's as far as we need to go. How many new converts are stranded on the wayside of life? How many are taught after their conversion? New converts are babies. They need to be taken by the hand, and they need to be spoon-fed.

Not only do we leave these young converts vulnerable to the vultures, but we also allow the wrong people to instruct them. Teachers who believe and practice things contrary to the word will teach things contrary to the word. One minister told me that we need to tolerate these liberal brethren. In other words, if we have someone teaching liberal doctrine, one should not cause friction by confronting them. We should let them teach. I genuinely do not see a difference in the philosophy from when I was in the charismatic movement. In that sect, we had different beliefs yet tolerated one another for the group's good.

False teachers are being praised as heroes today—men like Max Lucado, who has joined hands with denominationalism. He has become an ecumenical partner with Billy Graham. These false teachers have taken that which is holy and have thrown it to the dogs. They have compromised truth for a buck, and they have led a massive amount of people astray. It's time to wake up and smell the roses!

I am also concerned about the negativism expressed by some of our members. When I was first inducted into the movement, I came home one summer from college. My dad took me on a fishing trip. It was a beautiful day. It would have been enjoyable in the middle of the lake with my father in my younger years, but those days were gone. I started speaking to my dad about my charismatic experience. He became angry with me and asked, "What happened to cause you to leave the truth?"

I never told my father that day why I left, and long after my father passed, I can't remember giving him the answer to his question. I believe my reason is parallel to many others who leave the faith.

In my younger years as a member of the Lord's church, I was privileged to be with a group of people who enjoyed each other's company. As years passed, I began to hear people speak ill of the church. It usually started with some preacher they didn't like or some member who did them wrong. Even ministers were involved in this backbiting epidemic. It made me wonder, "How could these people be the true representation of Christ on this earth when they speak so badly about one another?" Preachers gossiping and members telling lies created a cancer within me that needed to be healed. My brethren, these things ought not to be!

It's hard to tell the world about the church when it is hidden. The Bible informs us that we should "let our light shine," not flicker on and off. When you find religious groups shining their lights brightly, it is fantastic that we have as many members as we do. These denominational groups are not sources of the true light. That is why it is imperative that we, ministers of truth, reflect the true character of Christ. If we do this, others will follow.

If we are going to try to prevent God's elect from falling away, we need to stop feeling sorry for ourselves. So often, we think that what we do is useless. We see denominational churches growing by leaps and bounds around us, and we ponder the point of trying. Gospel preachers are charged to preach the word (2 Tim. 4:1-4). We can plant the seed and water it, but it is God who gives the increase (1 Cor. 3:6). Every seed we plant has the possibility of blossoming. Therefore, we must not become weary in well-doing (Gal. 6:9).

Another problem so typical among our brethren is the formulation of clicks. I don't feel it is wrong to enjoy the company of close friends. However, it is wrong to find established groups that are more involved in politics than religion.

Power struggles within the Lord's church are typical. It is sad but true. To win souls, these oppositional groups need to be abolished. How? One may ask. The answer is found in the pages of the most sacred book, the Bible. Paul declared in 1 Corinthians 1:12-18 that it was wrong to formulate groups supporting one minister over another. This philosophy was dividing the church. Paul wants them to center their minds on Christ.

Ministers of the Gospel need to bring people back to reality. This demands that there must be unity in doctrine and commitment. God's people must remember that we can't drag people into a sinking ship. We must wave our flags high. We must prove to the world that we are who we are. This implies that we must exceed the charismatic when it comes to evangelism. When it comes to our living, we are to imitate Christ!

Instrumental Music in Worship

The charismatic movement often incorporates instrumental music into worship, turning services into high-energy events with drums, guitars, and amplified voices. While this may enhance the emotional experience of prayer, examining whether it aligns with biblical guidelines is essential.

Biblical Perspective:

The New Testament specifies that worship should be conducted with the heart, as seen in Ephesians 5:19 and Colossians 3:16, where singing and making melody in the heart to the Lord is emphasized. There is no New Testament command or example endorsing the use of mechanical instruments in worship.

Old Testament vs. New Testament:

Although the Old Testament includes various instruments in worship (e.g., Psalms), the New Testament reveals a shift away from these practices, as the Old Law has been fulfilled and replaced by the New Covenant (Galatians 3:19-27; Colossians 2:14).

Revelation 14:2:

Charismatics may cite Revelation 14:2, which mentions harpers with harps. However, this passage describes what John heard, not what was used in worship. The verse metaphorically describes a voice, not a literal use of harps in the worship of God.

The use of instruments in worship is often driven by personal preference rather than scriptural authority. According to the New Testament, true worship involves singing and making melody with the heart, focusing on spiritual rather than physical or emotional stimulation.

Spiritual Healings

Charismatics frequently cite personal experiences of miraculous healings to support their beliefs in ongoing spiritual gifts. They may recount stories of illness recovery or miraculous healings as evidence of God's continuing work.

Biblical Perspective:

During the New Testament era, miracles and healings were performed to authenticate the message of the gospel and the authority of Christ and His apostles. Examples include Jesus healing the sick instantly and without medical intervention (e.g., Luke 5:17-26).

Questions to Consider:

1. **Oral Roberts and Hospitals:**
   - If Oral Roberts could perform miraculous healings, why did he establish a hospital? This question challenges the idea that modern-day healers possess the same miraculous power as those in the New Testament.

2. **Verifiable Miracles:**
   - Have we witnessed verifiable instances of raising the dead, complete and instant healing of blindness, or other miracles without medical aid? Such questions test the authenticity of claims of spiritual healing.

New Testament Healing vs. Modern Claims:

In the New Testament, healing was instantaneous and complete. The lack of immediate, complete miracles in modern contexts contrasts with the biblical account, where healing was evident and unassisted by medical means.

Claims of modern spiritual healing should be critically examined in light of New Testament examples. The absence of verifiable, miraculous healings today suggests that these gifts were specific to the apostolic age and not intended to continue indefinitely.

Premillennialism

Premillennialism, a belief held by some charismatics, asserts that Jesus will return to establish a literal thousand-year kingdom on earth before the final judgment. This doctrine often includes a "rapture" where the righteous are taken to heaven, leaving the wicked on earth.

Biblical Perspective:

- **Kingdom Already Established:**
  - Jesus indicated that His kingdom was imminent, as seen in Matthew 16:17-18, where He promises to build His church. The kingdom's establishment was fulfilled during the New Testament era (Acts 1:8; 2:1-4; Colossians 1:13).
- **John's Testimony:**

- Revelation 1:9 describes John as being in the kingdom, indicating that the kingdom was already present during his time. This supports the view that the kingdom was established before the end of the first century.

Premillennialism's premise of a future, literal thousand-year kingdom contradicts the New Testament's teachings that the kingdom of God is already present and identified with the church. The rapture and second-chance doctrine concept also lacks direct biblical support, aligning more with interpretative frameworks rather than clear scriptural evidence.

Examining these doctrines through a scriptural lens helps clarify their alignment with biblical teachings and identify areas where personal preferences or misinterpretations may influence beliefs.

Building the Brotherhood

We must broaden our perspective and recognize that righteousness is not confined to our local congregations. Like Elijah, who initially thought he was the only righteous one left, we should remember that God has preserved many faithful believers. As He said to Elijah, "Yet I have left me seven thousand in Israel, all the knees which have not bowed unto Baal" (1 Kings 19:18).

To strengthen our community, we should:

- **Visit Other Congregations:** Attend gospel meetings and events at different congregations to build connections and support the broader church community.

- **Engage with Literature:** Invest in and read literature produced by brethren to gain insights and foster unity.

- **Involve Families:** Introduce your family and children to visiting ministers and get them involved in local church activities. Ensure that activities for young people are organized regularly.

This engagement helps counteract the influence of fanatical groups and reinforces the collective strength of the church, recognizing that Satan seeks to lead people astray (1 Peter 5:8).

Ten Steps to Follow

Maintain Clear Direction

Keep your focus on Christ and avoid letting others influence your spiritual direction. Your commitment to Christ should guide your path.

Remember the Basics

Never forget the foundational teachings of the church:

- The concept of one body and one head (Ephesians 1:22-23).

- God's plan of salvation.

- The five parts of worship on the Lord's Day.

These basics provide clarity and direction in your spiritual journey.

Resolve Conflicts Gracefully

Avoid walking away from conflicts in anger. Human imperfections can lead to disagreements but aim to resolve differences peacefully or part on amicable terms, hoping for reconciliation.

Recognize the Power of Satan

Be aware of Satan's tactics and avoid pride. Even the strongest individuals, like David and Solomon, were susceptible to his schemes. Stay vigilant.

Continue Growing

Spiritual growth is essential. Just as physical growth is a natural part of life, so is spiritual development. Feed your growth with the proper diet of God's word.

Be Active in Church Affairs

Engage actively in church activities. If opportunities seem lacking, take the initiative by starting Bible studies or other activities in your home. Don't wait for others to act.

Commit to Daily Study

Prioritize studying the Bible daily. This habit will become rewarding and fulfilling, helping you stay connected with God's word.

Stay Informed

Keep up with what is happening within the church and be prepared to refute false doctrines. Knowledge helps you live according to the truth.

Focus on the positive aspects of the church. Avoid negativity and remember that Jesus promised the church would prevail (Matthew 16:18). Surround yourself with uplifting influences.

Prioritize Prayer

Make prayer a regular part of your life. Pray for your family, yourself, and the church. Use prayer to connect with God and seek His guidance and support (James 5:16; 1 Thessalonians 5:17).

By following these steps, you can navigate the challenges of faith, contribute to a more substantial church community, and foster spiritual growth and resilience.

The Providence of God

1. Distinguishing Providence from Miracles

It's crucial to differentiate between a miracle and God's providence, as they are often used interchangeably, though they have distinct meanings in Biblical terms.

Definition of Providence:

Providence refers to God's ongoing governance and preservation of creation. It encompasses His involvement in every aspect of the universe—every falling star, every bird in flight, and every blooming tree. Providence reflects God's general care and control over the world, not necessarily through direct intervention but through His overarching plan.

Two words come to mind when speaking about miracles: instantaneous and immediate. Miracles showcase the direct power of God. Miracles were visible and undeniable, demonstrating God's power clearly and directly, such as the healings performed by Jesus and His apostles.

Understanding the Differences:

- **Power:** Miracles involve God's direct power and are visibly observed. For example, when Jesus healed a blind man or raised Lazarus from the dead, God's power was evident and immediate. Providence, however, works more subtly. When prayers for healing are answered over time, the process is less obvious, making it harder to attribute recovery directly to divine intervention.

- **Performance:** Miracles were performed publicly and were evident to all. Jesus and the apostles performed miracles openly, revealing their divine nature. Today, God's providence operates in ways that are less visible and harder to discern. Events such as natural disasters or disease outbreaks can be seen as part of God's providence, but it is not always clear if these are direct actions of God or the result of natural processes.

- **Person:** Miracles direct glory and attention to God as they manifest His power. In contrast, providence often operates naturally and may not always directly point to God. While God remains active and involved in the world, how His providence unfolds may not always be as apparent.

Providence in Practice

Providence is evident in how God sustains and interacts with creation, even if it isn't always obvious or directly attributable to His hand. For example:

- **Personal Experience:** The author recounts a personal experience of recovering from a high fever, attributing the recovery to God's providence. While such personal beliefs are deeply held, they cannot be empirically proven to others.

- **Job's Experience:** In the story of Job, his friends mistakenly attributed his suffering to God's wrath, while the actual cause was Satan's actions. This demonstrates that not all calamities are directly caused by God; sometimes, they are part of a larger spiritual battle or natural occurrences.

While God's providence is always at work in the world, it differs from the miraculous acts performed in biblical times. Miracles demonstrate divine power, while providence involves God's indirect involvement through natural processes and events. Understanding this distinction helps us recognize the ongoing role of God in our lives and the world, even if His actions are not always immediately visible or understandable.

Conclusion

Reflecting on my journey from the small dormitory room at Vincennes University to my office in Elkhart, Indiana, I am struck by the transformative power of faith and the trials that have shaped my path. This journey, spanning fifteen years as a gospel preacher, has been filled with challenges and triumphs. It has been a path of rediscovery, where I have had to re-educate myself and find a way to reconnect with the friends and community I once left behind. The road has been arduous, yet it has brought me to a place of renewed commitment and understanding.

I often recall the story of the prodigal son, which serves as a poignant metaphor for my own journey. Just as the prodigal son returned home to his father, I have found my way back to the core values and convictions that guide my faith. This return has not been without its trials. It has required deep introspection and a willingness to confront the missteps of the past. However, it has also given me a profound purpose and direction.

For those struggling with their faith or distant from their spiritual roots, my story serves as both a warning and an encouragement. The experience of returning to faith after a period of wandering underscores the importance of vigilance and dedication in our spiritual lives. It is all too easy to become complacent, to attend services sporadically, or to prioritize other activities over worship. Yet, these actions have real consequences, particularly for our children.

If we, as parents and church members, are not diligent in nurturing our spiritual lives, we risk exposing our children to the dangers of misguided doctrines and spiritual apathy. Our children are impressionable, and without a firm foundation of faith, they can easily be led astray. Many parents bear this burden, often too late, as they grapple with the consequences of their own spiritual neglect.

The urgency of our spiritual mission cannot be overstated. We must recognize the broader mission to reach others and strengthen the faith community as we navigate our journeys. The imagery of setting the woods on fire, a line from a song I remember, aptly captures the need for a passionate and vigorous pursuit of faith. It symbolizes the need to ignite a spiritual hunger that can spread throughout our communities and beyond.

Jesus' statement, "The harvest truly is plenteous, but the laborers are few" (Matt. 9:37), is a call to action for all of us.

The fields are ripe for harvest, meaning there is a significant need for dedicated individuals willing to work in God's service. The challenge we face is not merely about our personal faith but about actively participating in the spiritual renewal and outreach that our world so desperately needs.

To meet this challenge, we must be proactive in our efforts. This involves personal spiritual growth and a commitment to engaging with and supporting our faith communities. We need to be involved in church activities, contribute to our children's spiritual education, and reach out to those who may be lost or struggling. The church is not merely a place of worship; it is a living, dynamic community that thrives on the active participation of its members.

One practical step we can take is to invest time in understanding and addressing the needs of our local congregations. This means being attentive to the needs of our young people, ensuring they have opportunities for spiritual development and involvement. If we find that certain aspects of church life are lacking, it is our responsibility to take the initiative and make changes. Organizing Bible studies, youth activities, and outreach programs are all ways to contribute positively to the life of the church.

Moreover, being diligent in our studies and understanding of Scripture is crucial. In an age where misinformation and false doctrines can easily spread, it is imperative that we are well-informed and able to refute errors. This requires a commitment to daily Bible study and engagement with theological resources. By equipping ourselves with knowledge, we can better support our faith and help others navigate their spiritual journeys.

Maintaining a positive outlook on the church and its mission is also vital. Despite challenges and criticisms, we must remember the enduring promise that the church will prevail. Jesus assured us that "the gates of hell shall not prevail against it" (Matt. 16:18). This promise should encourage us to remain steadfast and optimistic, even in the face of difficulties.

Lastly, the power of prayer cannot be underestimated. Prayer is our direct line to God and a crucial element of our spiritual lives. Regular, heartfelt prayer supports not only our personal growth but also the broader mission of the church. We should pray for ourselves, our families, our church, and the world, asking for guidance, strength, and the courage to fulfill our spiritual responsibilities.

The journey from my early days of faith to my current role has been transformative and enlightening. It has reinforced the importance of dedication, proactive engagement, and a deep commitment to the spiritual well-being of ourselves and others. As we move forward, let us remember the lessons learned and the call to action that Jesus has given us. The harvest is ready, and the laborers are needed. It is time for us to rise, set our spiritual fires ablaze, and work diligently to build a stronger, more vibrant faith community. Let us carry our banners into battle, fully aware of the responsibility we bear and the potential for transformation that lies ahead.

88

Made in the USA
Columbia, SC
25 May 2025

58254210R00050